Albany James Christie

The Martyrdom Of St. Cecilia

A Drama In Three Acts

Albany James Christie

The Martyrdom Of St. Cecilia
A Drama In Three Acts

ISBN/EAN: 9783741156366

Manufactured in Europe, USA, Canada, Australia, Japa

Cover: Foto ©Thomas Meinert / pixelio.de

Manufactured and distributed by brebook publishing software
(www.brebook.com)

Albany James Christie

The Martyrdom Of St. Cecilia

THE MARTYRDOM OF ST. CECILIA.

ROEHAMPTON:

PRINTED BY JAMES STANLEY.

THE

MARTYRDOM OF ST. CECILIA.

A DRAMA

BY

ALBANY JAMES CHRISTIE,

S.J.

———

FOURTH EDITION.

———

LONDON:

BURNS, OATES, AND CO., PORTMAN STREET,

AND PATERNOSTER ROW.

———

1870.

DRAMATIS PERSONÆ.

—◆—

AZRAEL, Guardian Angel of Cecilia.
St. PETER.
URBAN.
MARCUS, a Priest.
VALERIAN.
METELLUS, father of Cecilia.
LEONIDAS, a Christian veteran.
ALMACHIUS, Prefect of Rome.
LUCIUS, a Roman soldier.
SOTER,
HERMES, } slaves of Valerian.
MUCRO,
Messenger.
Servant.

CECILIA.
METELLA, mother of Cecilia.
CHARIS, } slaves of Metellus.
MAURA,

SCENE—*Rome.*

THE
MARTYRDOM OF ST. CECILIA.

ACT THE FIRST.

SCENE I.

House of Metellus.

Enter CHARIS.

CHARIS.

ROME is in trouble; rumours are afloat
That once again the persecutor's rage
Is to assail the Church, and make the
road
To Heaven short but sharp. I have some
fears
We need the pruning-knife; this lull of
late
Has fostered lukewarmness, and charity
Is growing cool. We have big talkers, true,
Who boast that neither rack nor fire shall move
Their steadfast faith; but it needs a grace

B

Greater than common to persevere in good—
A grace beyond all merit, and which God
Gives not to pride, but to humility.
Such grace may He in mercy grant to me,
And to my dear young mistress Cecily!
The dazzling world, with all its specious gifts,
Is opening upon her, while the faith
Brings with it scorn and ignominious death.
But Cecily is humble; and, amid
So much to alarm, I fear not for the issue.

Enter MAURA.

MAURA.

So, Mistress Charis, pretty news for you;
You'll have to look about you.   Have you heard
The talk in Rome to-day?

CHARIS.

In part, I think;
I've heard the Emperor is about to leave
Rome for the provinces.

MAURA.

And thereby hangs a tale.
Severus has been soft, and let alone

The pests of Rome, and they have multiplied—
Your Christian vermin. But, when he is gone,
Apollo and the gods shall deal with them
As they deserve.

CHARIS.

Nay, Maura; don't be hard
Upon us. Have you suffered aught of ill
From me or any of the Christian name?

MAURA.

No; I don't say I have. And—I take it—
The reason is, because you are so mean
And drivelling-spirited, that you dare not do
What men of spirit dare.

CHARIS.

Then you prefer
A man of spirit that would do you wrong,
To men who only wish to do you good?

MAURA.

Why, yes, I do! I cannot bear your shams,
Your downcast eyes, and modest garb, forsooth!
Your want of courage to resent a wrong.
Why! were a man to strike you on the cheek,

B 2

I do believe that you would turn your face
That he might smite the other.

CHARIS.

Six months ago
You were attacked with fever, Maura ; I too
Lay burning, restless, parched with torturing thirst.
What comfort then was ours ?

MAURA.

What d'ye mean ?
What, Charis, has our fever, then, to do
With Christian drivelling ?

CHARIS.

Nay, tell me, Maura,
What comfort had we then ?   Did Martha help you ?

MAURA.

Ay, did she !   Yes ; when all the others fled,
And shunned us both, and would have let us die
Like dogs, uncared for and untended, she
Lived but for us : the live-long day she spent
At my couch or at yours ; our fretfulness—
Nay, mine, not yours—she bore, and seemed to know

By instinct every want ; she brought your couch
Into my cell, that even all night long,
Sleepless herself, she might, with loving care,
Supply our wants ; and while she cared for us,
She took the fever, and, as I grew well,
She sank and died.

CHARIS.

And was this cowardice
And drivelling spirit, Maura ?   Nay, I could tell
Something of Martha that you know not of,
But that I fear that you would mock at it,
And call it folly.

MAURA.

Nay, tell me, Charis.
I will not mock ! for Martha died for me,
And so I cannot mock.

CHARIS.

Martha, your nurse and mine,
Was, though you knew it not, a Christian. When you
Were lying at your worst, and I just then
Was mending, and to Martha seemed asleep,
I heard her offer to the Christian's God
Her life for yours in earnest, heart-poured prayer.
She saw you trembling on the very verge

Of that eternity which you think not of,
And knew your peril. She prayed that she might die,
And you be spared.

MAURA.

                    And wherefore, Charis ?
What, did she wish to make a Christian of me ?
To feast on human flesh ? deny the gods ?
Worship an ass's head ?   Alas, poor Martha !
Her heart was full of goodness ; but 'tis pity
That so much goodness should be spoiled and marred
By follies like the Christian.

CHARIS.

                    Yet, 'twas Christian folly
That saved your life, and made the blessed Martha
Martyr of charity.   Maura, I entreat you
Do not believe those monstrous practices
That others palm on us are really ours.
It is a cunning trick of evil men,
By whom the people are deceived, to assert
That we believe and do the very things
Which we abhor.—Now, I must go and seek
The Lady Cecily ; so farewell, Maura,
Till dinner-time.   Our lady bade me tell you
To go to her at mid-day ; she is in her room. [*Exeunt.*

SCENE II.

𝕮𝖊𝖈𝖎𝖑𝖎𝖆'𝖘 𝕮𝖍𝖆𝖒𝖇𝖊𝖗.

CECILIA, *with a chorus of Angels, sings the Hymn of St. Thecla.*

HAIL to thee, Thecla! Asia's land
    Boasts thee, its earliest rose,
First of the Virgin-Martyr band
    Slain for their heavenly Spouse.
Iconium nursed thy tender years,
    Rear'd thee to womanhood,
Saw, when Paul preached, thy contrite tears,
    And laid thee in thy shroud.

Hail to thee, Thecla! Worldly pride,
    And Plato's dreamy lore,
Wealth, that thy ev'ry want supplied,
    All held thee in their power.
But, from the first, thy heart was kept
    Pure in the midst of sin;
God for His service saw thee apt,
    And chose thee for His shrine.

Hail to thee, Thecla! When St. Paul
 Proclaim'd the Word of God,
Thou didst renounce wealth, rank, and all,
 And seal thy faith in blood.
Around thee roar'd the crackling flame,
 Wild lions licked thy feet,
And Jesus to thy rescue came
 With the choice coronet.

CECILIA.

O Thecla, Virgin Martyr! how I grieve
I cannot show my love for my dear Lord
As thou hast done! The times are changed, and
  peace
Has reigned well-nigh unbroken since the day
Septimius died. Sweet Saint, I envy thee;
I can for Christ do nothing : wealth surrounds me,
And all I need I have. I sometimes fear
God is not pleased with me; for whom He loves
He chasteneth.

      Enter CHARIS.

CHARIS.

Dear Lady Cecily——

CECILIA.

What, Charis! will you never learn to speak
As I have taught you?   "Lady" before the world;
But when we are alone, you call me "sister."

CHARIS.

True, dearest sister; but the news I bring
Quite frightened me from my propriety.

CECILIA.

Is't good or bad?   I cannot read your looks.

CHARIS.

Why, good and bad; which most, I cannot tell:
The good news is, that you and I may yet
Have our prayers answered, and be called to seal
Our faith in blood.   The bad news is,
Your noble parents are resolved to urge
Valerian's suit, and make you marry him.

CECILIA.

What think you, Charis?   It would seem that God
Has with the poison sent the antidote.
The bad news shall be frustrate by the good—
Wedlock by martyrdom.   But, be more precise,

Leave out the bad ; noble Valerian's suit
Is an old suit new-urged ; but what you hint
Of suff'ring for the faith is, in these easy days,
News worth the telling.

CHARIS.

They say the Emperor
Severus has this morning quitted Rome,
And left Almachius Prefect, who is bent
On putting into force the penal laws
Against the Christians, which have slept for years.
Mammæa, Empress-Mother, who so long
Has by her kindly influence restrained
The passions of the mob, that many a one
Suspects that she herself is of the faith—
She now is powerless ; and the infidels
Egg on the willing Prefect to compel
The Christians to burn incense to the gods.

CECILIA.

O joyful news ! So, then, I need not wait
Till age or sickness brings me to the grave ;
But, it may be, before a week is out
I may behold the glory of my Lord.

CHARIS.

Pray too for me, dear sister : as on earth
I have attended you, and loved you well,
Pray that in death I may attend you too,
And share your crown.

Enter METELLA *and* MAURA.

METELLA.

Cecily, my child,
Your father wishes me to speak with you.

CECILIA.

What is it, dearest mother ?   I am here,
Ready to listen, and, as I hope, obey.

METELLA.

Why "as I hope," my child ? you never used
To speak as though obedience could be hard
Or questionable.

CECILIA.

Charis just now has told me
Valerian has urged his suit again,
And that my father, and that you, dear mother,
Would have me wed him.

METELLA.

Well, it is so, my child ;
And wherefore not ?   What is there in Valerian
Displeases you ?

CECILIA.

Valerian is brave
And noble-hearted—has every manly virtue ;
His gentleness gives to each action grace ;
He is a most accomplished gentleman,
Worthy of honour, and my best esteem.
He lacks no gift of nature ; open-browed
And open-handed, frank and generous ;
Fit ornament of the Imperial Court,
Yet condescending to the weak and poor.

METELLA.

I came to praise Valerian, Cecily,
And you have praised him more than I could do.
Why, then, refuse his hand ?

CECILIA.

What can I say ?
You are my mother.   I would do all I can
To make you happy.   I am in a strait :

In this one point I thwart you, and despair
Of finding reasons which might aught avail
To make you think as I do.   Do not urge
Valerian's suit, dear mother.   Never yet
Have I had cause to grieve thee ; do not urge
The state of wedlock on a girl who feels
She is averse to it.

METELLA.

You are a riddle, child !
Here is a match that any Roman lady
Would be most proud of.   You yourself confess
Valerian's worth ; your father and myself
Feel the advantages of this alliance,
And all Rome sees the love and the respect
Valerian shows you.   This is perverseness, Cecily !
Your father will not bear it, nor can I.
I shall report to him the ill-success
That I have met with ; and you must expect
The sternness of his strict authority.

[*Exit with Maura.*

CECILIA.

My mother—she is gone.   Leave me for a while,
Dear Charis ; go and pray for me.   You know
My reasons well : 'twas you made known to me

Another Spouse, whose dwelling is on high ;
Whose love has made Him do so much for me,
I cannot share the love I bear to Him.

CHARIS.

He will support thee, sister ; thou hast need
Not now of human help, but of divine.
I know where thou wilt seek it—seek it there,
And thou shalt find it.

[*Exit.*

CECILIA [*alone*].

God bless thee, Charis !
Yes, God will bless her—my playfellow and friend.
We have grown up together, she a slave,
And I a daughter of nobility.
Then, as we lived together, and I saw
Her modesty and charity, I soon learned
There needed more than all my parents knew
To make her what she was.   I was her scholar ;
And the poor slave told the proud Roman lady
Of things that made her feel her littleness,
And taught her what true greatness is.   She told
Of God becoming Man, and crucified ;
And how God-Man dwells still, in love, with men

In the blest Sacrament.   There is His Sacred Heart:
His Heart is mine, and mine is wholly His ;
And in the wilderness of this vast palace,
Where slaves in hundreds serve, and worldly pomp
Shines in its proudest guise—where I can find
No sympathy from dearest parents—still
I have my refuge and my comfort near ;
And now I go to seek it.   Lucina's house
Is privileged : Urban, the blessed Pope,
Allows Lucina in a private chapel
To keep the Blessed Sacrament.   Above the altar
There hangs a silver dove ; in it is shrined
The Holiest : there I shall gather strength
To do the will of God.   In the very presence
Of Him Whose Birth, and Death, and Resurrection
Is in this book of the holy Gospel writ,

     [Brings out from her bosom the roll of the holy Gospel.

I shall gain strength to live and die as He,
My Master and my Spouse.

     Sweet music.   Enter AZRAEL.

AZRAEL.

Cecilia, fear not ; I am ever with thee,

Though hitherto unseen.   I'll go with thee,
Into our Master's presence ; and thou shalt find
Grace for the time of trial.

CECILIA.

                    Blest Guardian Spirit,
I cannot fear when I do look on thee,
And see thy goodness in thy countenance.
So thou art he whom I have daily asked
To guard and guide me ! But wherefore hast thou now
Made thyself visible to eyes of flesh ?

AZRAEL.

                    To thee alone
Shall I be visible ; to others not.
It is the will of God thine eyes should see me,
Because He hath reserved to thee a trial
Strange and unwonted.

CECILIA.

                    Blessed be His name !
And what is it, dear Angel ? for my heart
Is fain to know it.   My heart expands with hope :
I know it will not be beyond my strength ;
For He is with me, sending me thy aid.

AZRAEL.

It is His will, Cecilia, that thou wed
Valerian, who wooes thee : yet both he and thou
Shall win the special crown which virgins wear
In the bright court of Heaven.

CECILIA.

His will be done!
How this shall be, His wisdom will provide ;
Meanwhile, thy presence is a certain pledge
Of His o'erwatching care.

AZRAEL.

Now, let us go
And make this visit thou wast purposing :
Come, and renew to Him within the dove
Thy constant promise of fidelity.

[Exeunt

C

SCENE III.

House of Metellus.

Enter METELLUS *and* METELLA.

METELLUS.

METELLA, there is that in Cecily
Puzzles us both.

METELLA.

Yes, truly! she is at once
Yielding and stubborn.   Yet her stubbornness
Is with such gentleness maintained, that one
Scarce dares to call her stubborn.

METELLUS.

Strangest of all!
That very point wherein you call her stubborn,
She yields at once.

METELLA.

What! do you mean to say
That she will wed Valerian?

METELLUS.

Not a word

Said she against it.

METELLA.

And did you show yourself
Stern and resolved ?   Was it through fear she spoke ?

METELLUS.

No ; I began as gently as I could—
Even pretending to take part with her.
When I had done, she said all modestly,
She loved Valerian, and esteemed him highly ;
And that she knew no hindrance in the way
Of the alliance that I came to urge.

METELLA.

She is as strange in this her yielding mood
As ever in her stubbornness before.

METELLUS.

She seems to act unreasonably ; yet
She has her reasons, could we get at them.
However, 'tis the match we look to, wife ;
And Cecily is Valerian's for life.

C 2

Enter SERVANT.

SERVANT.

My Lord Valerian asks to see you, sir.

METELLUS.

Let him come in.

[*Exit Servant.*

        I'm growing young again ;
We will secure, Metella, Briso's farm,
Add a few hundred acres to our park,
And buy a thousand slaves ; why, woman, why
We'll build an amphitheatre ; I'll be Consul,
And get the government of Syria !
Who knows but we may aim still higher ?   Men
Below myself in rank, not half so rich
As I shall be, have mounted to the throne,
And worn the imperial purple.

METELLA.

      Hush, husband ; hush !
Here comes Valerian ; he will hear the use
We mean to put his loaded coffers to.

Enter VALERIAN.

METELLUS.

Well met, Valerian ! Everything is done ;
Our Cecily is yours, and you are ours.

METELLA [*aside*].

That is, his money is ; as for himself,
We could do well without him. [*To Valerian*] Noble son—
For so I'll call you now—we welcome you.

VALERIAN.

The gods be thanked ! I am amazed, 'tis true ;
But sink amazement in my gratitude.
I am not worthy of your daughter. You,
By your kind mediation, must have won
My cause, and Cecily's consent.

METELLA.

'Tis true
We both have done our best.

METELLUS.

Nothing remains,
So far as I can see, but name the day ;

And let it be as early as you can.
When shall it be?

VALERIAN.

If Cecily would not think
To-morrow fortnight sign of too much haste——

METELLUS.

Trust us for that: to-morrow fortnight, son,
Shall be the day.

VALERIAN.

Meanwhile, so great my joy,
I will set free a hundred of my slaves,
And gladden all the widows' hearts in Rome.
Twenty poor maidens I'll give portions to,
And feast my tenants on my wedding-day
As they shall ne'er forget it ; and all this
'Tis Cecily does, not I.   Tell her, for her sake
So many hearts shall beat with joy in Rome.

METELLUS [*aside*].

By Bacchus! he'll spend all his money.   [*To
    Valerian*] Son,
Be not imprudent in your largesses ;
Money, when given, bears no interest.

VALERIAN.

Metellus, I would fain do ten times more;
Pray hinder not my joy; I'd rather be
A poor man, with your daughter, than without her
Wallow in riches.

METELLUS.

                Ay, but consider her;
You must not make her poor, however much
Your young imagination may encase
A hovel, shared with Cecily, with gold,
Which will not bear the touchstone.

VALERIAN.

                You are right;
For sake of Cecily I'll make others rich;
For sake of Cecily I'll be rich myself.
Farewell! my brother is without, expecting me;
My happiness is his; he will rejoice
At my good fortune like another self,
And I seem selfish till I share with him
My happiness. Greet your noble daughter,
And bless her for her graciousness to me.

                      [Exeunt.

SCENE IV.

𝕿𝖍𝖊 𝕳𝖔𝖚𝖘𝖊 𝖔𝖋 𝕬𝖗𝖇𝖆𝖓.

URBAN *alone.*

URBAN.

THE wolves already raven in the flock,
    And tear my sheep and lambs. I can but pray
    That all and each may persevere and win
    The crown of martyrdom. O my dearest
        children,
    May the good God support you! Sharp the
        strife ;
    But while the persecutors rage, and hell
    Sends forth its myrmidons, your Guardian
        Spirits
Float still around you, bearing in their hands
The palm of victory and the wreath of glory,
Which one rude stroke will make for ever yours.

Enter CECILIA *and* CHARIS: *they kneel.*

God's blessing be upon you, children ; welcome!
More now than ever.

CECILIA.

Most holy Father,
You are in danger here.

URBAN.

Danger, my child ?
And are not you in danger too ?

CECILIA.

Father, you must fly ;
The Pagans know this place, and they will seek
Among the first the shepherd of the flock.

URBAN.

Yet, Cecily, you know you would be glad
If I received the grace of martyrdom !

CECILIA.

Yes, Father, but that all depend on you,
And need your help to persevere in good.

URBAN.

God can provide, as He has done till now ;
E'en Peter's self could die and not be missed.

Enter a MESSENGER.

MESSENGER.

Upon the Appian Road, three miles from Rome,
There is a dying woman.   She was seized
And carried to the Prefect as a Christian.
Beaten with rods and torn with hooks, at last
She fainted, and was left for dead.   At night
Some of the Faithful found her breathing still,
And have conveyed her to the Catacombs
Upon the Appian Way.   She seemed to rally,
But now is sinking fast.

URBAN.

               I will come,
And you shall guide me.   Farewell, Cecily ;
And farewell, Charis.

                    [*Exit, with Messenger.*

CECILIA.

His charity shall save his life.   'Twas vain
To urge him for himself; but now he's gone
Out of the city, we will do our best
To keep him in security.   Charis, go
And fetch Leonidas the veteran.   Tell him

I've work for him I would not trust to many;
Tell him to come at once.

CHARIS.

He's somewhere in the house,
And I shall find him soon.   [*Exit.*

CECILIA [*alone*].

The storm is thickening,
And every hour as it passes brings,
As I would humbly hope, the moment nearer
When I shall gaze on Him Who died for me.
Martyrs now count by thousands; I am left
As still unworthy of that priceless gift.
This very morning has a playmate winged
Her flight to Heaven.   O most blest Martina,
Virgin and martyr! little knew the judge
The grace within thee when he bade thee burn
The incense to Apollo; when he plied
The iron hooks and rent thy tender flesh,
Then the raw wounds with broken potsherds scraped—
He little knew the power of the One,
Who, coming in the Blessed Sacrament,
Made of thy body His most sacred shrine.

What though the executioners grew tired,
Dealing their blows on thee, and thrice were changed?
The thought of His dire scourging was enough
To hold thee up.   What though the melted fat
Was poured upon thy body, and the flame
Scorched thee so sharply ? thou wast all unmoved,
Like the three children in the blazing fire:
Thy Lord was by, and nerved thy heart and soul
With firmness to the end and perfect peace.
We used to study and to play together,
And thou hast taught me many a blessed way
Of ministering to Jesus in His poor.
Had I made better progress, it may be
I might, in dying too, have lived with thee.

Enter CHARIS *with* LEONIDAS.

CHARIS.

At last I've found him ; he was catechising
Three little children in the garden.

LEONIDAS.
                                        Lady,
How can I serve you ?

CECILIA.

The Holy Father
Is gone to tend a dying woman. Go,
Tell the Priest Marcus and the Deacon Leo,
Who are secreted near the Latin Gate,
And bid them hasten to the Catacombs,
And press the Holy Father all they can
Not to return just now to Rome, but stay
In private there : they know the reasons well.
If they prevail, then you, Leonidas,
Station yourself upon the Appian Road,
Nearest the Catacomb, and let no man know
Where Urban is, unless he give the pass-word.
If Marcus think it good, the word may be,
"Our Master watches."   Haste, Leonidas ;
The Holy Father's life depends on thee.

LEONIDAS.

God bless thee, lady ; pray for good success.

[*Exeunt.*

END OF THE FIRST ACT.

ACT THE SECOND.

SCENE I.

Valerian's House.

MUCRO *and* SOTER.

MUCRO.

I TELL you what, Soter: if you were not a fellow-slave, I'd inform against you.

SOTER.

Well, Mucro, then it's an ill wind that blows nobody good: some good comes of being a slave. But what would be your charge?

MUCRO.

Why, that you're a Christian.

SOTER.

And, pray, how do you know that I'm a Christian?

MUCRO.

To be sure, it's rather soon to have found it out ; but for all that, I'm sure of it.

SOTER.

Well, now, just for the curiosity of the thing, let us see how you will prove it.

MUCRO.

First, you wouldn't get drunk on your first night here. Now I never knew an honest Pagan slave who feared the gods, who wouldn't get drunk whenever he had the chance.

SOTER.

Nay, Mucro, I've known some men who feared the gods, who never got drunk because wine didn't agree with them.

MUCRO.

Wine not agree with them! Don't tell me. Wine agrees with everybody ; and none but your sneaking Christians object to taking even what's called too much of it. Too much of it, indeed! I wonder what "too much" of it means? I've never had too much of it; and yet I've been found in the gutter at least once a fortnight for the last twelve months.

SOTER.

Ah, Mucro, that accounts for the pains in your limbs, I fear, and the narrow escape you had six months ago (as I heard in the country) of your changing this upper air for the gloomy regions.

MUCRO.

Well, certainly, there might have been a little too much, but only a little. And, perhaps, if I could have gone on taking more I shouldn't have suffered as I did.

SOTER.

You'd have died outright, and gone to see what the next world is like.

MUCRO.

No unlucky words, if you please, Soter; don't talk about the next world. I somehow feel all-overish when I think about it; then glorious wine sets me right again.

SOTER.

Then again all-overish when you get up in the morning, eh, Mucro?

MUCRO.

Enough! Let's change the subject. I'll give you another proof that you're a Christian. Yesterday Hermes behaved ill to you; now you're twice as strong as he, and you didn't knock him down.

SOTER.

Well, after all, if I am twice as strong as he, it would be hardly fair to knock him down.

MUCRO.

No, not in a pitched battle; but by way of chastising him, you might. It's fair, at least so say the gentry, for a dozen of policemen to take up one slave and flog him, though the policemen have the strength on their side. Now, if I had been in your place, I'd have pommelled Hermes till I had knocked the breath out of his body.

SOTER.

And I wonder who would have been best off—you after thrashing him, or I as I am now?

D

MUCRO.

Why I, to be sure : he'd think twice before he ever offended me again ; and in case I showed my teeth, he'd be off in no time, like a bolt from a cross-bow.

SOTER.

He would have feared you, but there'd have been no good-fellowship between you. What do you think? This same Hermes this morning, when he saw me dead tired with my work, brought me a cordial, and you can't think how glad he seemed to help me, and how happy I felt at having made him my friend.

MUCRO.

Bah! it's all hypocrisy. He wants to get something out of you ; and if you trust to people's generosity, you'll be a fool for your pains.

Enter HERMES.

HERMES.

Soter, you are free. Valerian bids you go to him to-morrow, that he may go through the regular form of giving you your liberty.

SOTER.

Why, how's this, Hermes?

HERMES.

The fact is, Valerian has just been accepted by the noblest and best lady in Rome—Cecilia, the daughter of Metellus; and he's so happy about it, that he's bent on making everybody else happy.

MUCRO.

What, then, are we all free?

HERMES.

Ah, Mucro, I didn't see you :—no, not all; but he frees a hundred; and he made the steward draw up a list of the most deserving.

MUCRO.

I wonder what "the most deserving" means? I wonder whether I come into that number?

HERMES.

The steward is something of a friend of mine, and he called me up to help him in making out the list.

D 2

MUCRO.

And you mentioned Soter, and left me out?

HERMES.

Not exactly. I mentioned Soter first, certainly, and you know I had reason to do so; but after securing his name, I confess, though it went rather against my conscience, yet, for old acquaintance sake, I named Mucro.

MUCRO.

You did, did you? and yet, from your way of talking, I can't flatter myself, I fear, that I am free.

HERMES.

No, Mucro; the steward looked surprised at me, and wondered how I could think of you. He said you were fitter for the gallows than for freedom, and began to suspect my recommendation of Soter; so I was obliged to tell him how shamefully I had treated Soter, and how well he had behaved to me, or I should have failed in both.

MUCRO.

I say, Soter; I said if you were not a fellow-slave,

I'd inform against you. I tell you what, Christian, if you get your freedom, and leave me behind, I *will* accuse you, and we'll see who'll be best off—Mucro in his slavery, or Soter with the lions.

SOTER.

God bless you, Mucro! You are right. Yes! I am a Christian; and if you accuse me, you will do me a better turn than you ever did comrade before.

HERMES.

Well, now, if I might venture my humble opinion, I don't think that's saying much. Mucro, who knows, perhaps you'll have to inform against me some day; for if it's Christianity has made Soter what he is, there must be something in it.

MUCRO.

A brace of fools. I'll have my revenge.

[*Exit.*

SOTER.

Hermes, I do not think that thou art far
From faith in the true God. Mucro is gone,
And will accuse me; let us use the time

As best we may.   I will declare to you
The Christian's faith ; and if I'm taken from you,
I will direct you where you may obtain
Further instruction.

HERMES.

You are unmoved by fear
Of Mucro's purpose.   You may this very day
Be thrown to the wild beasts.

SOTER.

If so, I die
For One Who offered up His life for me,
To win me bliss for all eternity.

[*Exeunt.*

SCENE II.

House of Metellus.

CHARIS *alone.*

CHARIS.

THIS world would be a riddle, did not faith
Enable us to penetrate the sham
And see the truth. The wicked seem to
    prosper,
The good to suffer; nay, among the good,
Some seem to suffer, and some seem to rest
In luxury and undisturbed repose.
Faith opens to our eyes the world to come,
The hollowness of all the joys of sin,
And benefit of suffering; and an accident
May show us how the noble and the rich
Make up for ease by suffering self-imposed.
While I prepared the wedding-ornaments
Of Cecily, the child of luxury,
I found by chance—what she had kept concealed
Even from me, who knew her every thought—
A bristling shirt of hair, which, next her skin,

She wore beneath her rich embroidered robes :
It had grown old, and ceased to vex so much
As Cecily desired ; and her wedding-day
She counts a fitting opportunity
To reassume the sharpness of the pain.
I found her sleeping ; and I could not spare
To satisfy my curiosity,
And see if she had put aside the penance
In honour of her marriage, or had changed
Rough pain for rougher ; and, as I imagined,
I found her skin all fretted with the bristles
Of a new hair-cloth.

Enter CECILIA *and* AZRAEL.

CHARIS.

Sister, 'tis almost time
To expect Valerian. All the guests are come,
And every tongue is lauding to the skies
Valerian's princely generosity.

CECILIA.

He does deserve their praises. You must pray,
Dear Charis, that a soul so richly 'dowed

With gifts of nature may be raised by grace
To Christian childlikeness.

CHARIS.

I'm sure that you
Have prayed for him, and offered many an act
Of penance for him.

CECILIA.

Of penance, Charis?
God knows how weak and cowardly I am
When I but think of penance and of pain ;
But that I know that God can nerve the weak,
Even the weakest, I should shake with fear
At each new rumour of a Christian slain.
Still you are right in thinking all I do .
Is done with longing that Valerian
May know God's truth. He'd make a noble Christian.

Enter METELLA *and* MAURA.

METELLA.

Come, Cecily ; you keep us waiting. Well,
You do us credit ; Valerian need not think
That he is condescending when he leads
Cecilia for his wife.

CECILIA.

I am ready, mother;
And you shall take me to the banquet-hall.
Come, Charis; come with us.

METELLA.

No, Cecily;
For reasons known to me and to your father,
Charis will not go with you; she remains
With us: we cannot spare her. You will have
Slaves and to spare in your new home. Come on!

CECILIA.

Oh, this would be a bitter grief, dear mother!
I never dreamed of living without Charis.

METELLA.

It must be so, and you must leave her here.
You have allowed her too much liberty;
She will forget that she is still a slave.

CECILIA.

Has she in aught shown a rebellious spirit,
That you should punish me in keeping her?

METELLA.

No; but prevention is the better cure;
And you must think no more about her.   Charis,
Go to the kitchen; I have told the cook
The work that you're to do.

CHARIS.

Lady, I go.

[Exit.

CECILIA.

Oh, what a gentle spirit have you bruised,
Dear mother, in those words!   Is it your will
I cease to plead for her?

METELLA.

Yes, child; yes.
You shall have Maura, if you want a slave;
But Charis is to stop.   Come, make haste;
We're wasting time.   Valerian is come.
Come, child, away!

[Exeunt.

SCENE III.

Valerian's House.

VALERIAN, CECILIA, AZRAEL.

VALERIAN.

THE din and bustle of the day is over;
And I have noted, Cecily, thy patience,
Which sweetly kept concealed the irksomeness
That wearied thee at heart.

CECILIA.

          Valerian,
Thou too, no less than I, art wearied out
With boisterous mirth; but there's another reason
Which made me feel the hours lag along,
And wish the banquet ended.

VALERIAN.

              Cecily, what was that?
Thy mien is changing: thou dost almost seem
Higher than earthly! Ever my love for thee
Was sanctioned by respect; but now I gaze
On thee with awe and wondering reverence.

CECILIA.

Valerian, I am a Christian.

VALERIAN.

                    A Christian, Cecily!
Then Christians cannot be the villain sect
That others make them.   I'm sure thy noble soul
Would shrink from all dishonour, and abhor
The filthy orgies men do charge them with.

CECILIA.

You do us justice : ever generous hearts
Keep time together.   Trust me, highest lore
Of man's philosophy is short of that
Which Christian children lisp and women know,
As finite falleth short of infinite ;
And Christian virtue does exceed the span
Of heathen practice, as the mid-day sun
Bathes in its light the twinkling stars of heaven,
And wholly drowns them.

VALERIAN.

                    Thyself art the best proof
Of that thou speakest ; and, in our life together,

No harm shall reach thee that my arm can ward,
But thou shalt worship as thy conscience bids,
Uninterfered by me.

CECILIA.

　　　　　I'm not surprised,
Valerian, at thy words : I know thee generous,
And generous deeds are done by thee of course.
Yet listen further : He, Whose name we bear,
Hath taught us, that while marriage is a blest
And holy state, still, they who love God most
Will, for the love that He has shown for them,
Give themselves wholly to Him and renounce
The entanglements of life.　The Lord my God
Hath chosen me to consecrate myself
This way to Him ; and—hear me, Valerian—
There standeth at my side, unseen by thee,
But seen by me, a heavenly Guardian Spirit,
Whom the Eternal has empowered to keep
Strict watching o'er me.

VALERIAN.

　　　　　More and more wondrous still !
I cannot disbelieve thee, yet thy words

Pass all belief. Cecily, I would see
This Guardian Spirit.

CECILIA.

As thou art now, my spouse,
Thou canst not see him ; God might grant the boon,
Wert thou admitted to the Christian fold,
And thy soul purified from nature's stain.

VALERIAN.

A mist seems peeling from my eyes; I feel
An inward drawing to the slandered faith
Of men who bear fierce pains with constancy,
Who so much love each other, and, not least,
Who are regarded by the most pure soul
Of Cecily as brethren. Tell me what to do ;
At least I'll make the trial.

CECILIA.

Go, my spouse,
Three miles along the Appian Way. When there,
Look for an old man named Leonidas,
And give the pass-word. He will guide you straight
To him whom God has given for our chief,

Urban, our Holy Father.   He will tell thee
What next to do.

CECILIA appears as VALERIAN.

VALERIAN.

'Twixt hope and fear I go.
What is the pass-word ?

CECILIA.

'Tis—" Our Master watches."
May the good God of Heaven guide thy steps,
And bring thee back in safety !

VALERIAN.

Till then farewell !

[*Exit.*

AZRAEL.

Spend thou the interval in prayer : meanwhile
I will repair to Heaven's presence-chamber,
And in thy name beg Mary and the Saints,
And all my brother Spirits, to implore
Grace and conversion for Valerian.

[*Exit.*

CECILIA.

No ill foreboding hovers round my heart :
Valerian too shall act the martyr's part.

SCENE IV.

The Appian Road.

LEONIDAS *alone.*

LEONIDAS.

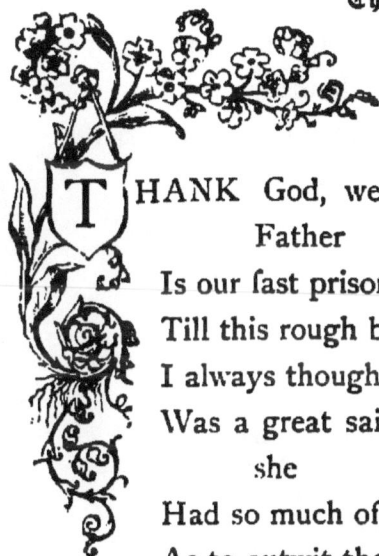

THANK God, we've got him safe! The Holy
    Father
Is our fast prisoner, and he sha'n't get out
Till this rough blast is over. Well, I'm sure
I always thought that Lady Cecily
Was a great saint ; but who'd have thought that
    she
Had so much of the woman in her, so much tact,
As to outwit the Pope! Ah! there he is,
Safe in the Catacombs, and not a friend
To help him out ; not one to pity him,
Or heed his prayers to let him go to Rome
And die like common Christians. To be sure,
There's so much pleasure in a harmless trick
To do another good, that old Leonidas
Feels like a boy again. But who comes here?
Urban is safely housed ; but I must see
No dangerous visitor find his whereabouts.

E

Enter VALERIAN.

VALERIAN.

Here is the milestone which should mark the spot
I had to look for.   Hereabouts should be
The watcher keeping guard. [*Sees Leonidas.*] Friend,
    who are you ?

LEONIDAS.

Why, sir, but you're a gentleman, I'd ask,
Pray who are you ?

VALERIAN.

                True, friend ; I was abrupt :
Let haste excuse me.

LEONIDAS.

                No offence, my lord ;
For now I see that you're a nobleman.
A pleasant journey to you !

VALERIAN.

                Stay, my friend——

LEONIDAS.

Nay, good my lord, I'm in a hurry too,
And cannot stay to parley.

VALERIAN.

I have cause
To ask thee who thou art.

LEONIDAS.

Have you, my lord?
And perhaps I've reason also not to tell you.

VALERIAN.

Pray, is thy name Leonidas?

LEONIDAS.

My name
"Leonidas?" Sure that's no Roman name,
And how can it be mine?

VALERIAN.

Would thou couldst trust
My honesty as I do thine. Tell me:
Are there not some about this neighbourhood
Have friends in Rome?

LEONIDAS.

Most likely, I should think;
'Tis only three miles off.

E 2

VALERIAN.

But are there none
Kept quiet here for fear of things in Rome?

LEONIDAS.

I do not think so: what have they to fear?

VALERIAN.

Why there is trouble in the city there,
And deaths are frequent.

LEONIDAS.

True; but where's the fear?
I'm told that they are Christians who are slain,
And Christians, they do say, fear not to die.
But what is that to you or me? Good night.

VALERIAN.

God grant I may not risk the pass-word rashly!
Friend, "Our Master watches."

LEONIDAS. '

What!—pardon me, my lord—
And you a Christian?

VALERIAN.

You, Leonidas,
Have done your part right faithfully; no need
Of pardon from me. Guide me instantly
To Urban: our parley has delayed us. Say
I come from Lady Cecily.

LEONIDAS.

Well! I'm sure
There's something here I cannot understand;
But I can trust you. Not many noblemen
Think it worth while to come so far alone
To see a poor old man; but you've good cause
I'm sure to do it. Come this way, my lord.

[*Exeunt.*

SCENE V.

𝔗𝔥𝔢 𝔆𝔞𝔱𝔞𝔠𝔬𝔪𝔟𝔰.

URBAN *alone.*

URBAN.

MY kind and cruel children, an old man
Such as myself might surely be allowed
To end a life (whose years e'en now are
          numbered)
A little sooner, by a sacrifice
Which would enrol me in the white-robed host
Of martyrs for the faith. I long to be dissolved
And be with Christ ; but I am told with tears—
Tears that have mastered me—that for the sake
Of weaker brethren, who in danger stand
Of shipwreck in their faith, I must awhile
Forego the bliss of dying. Hither repair
The catechumen and the fearful soul
For teaching and encouragement. Again,
Thus underground, amid the martyred dead,
The Faithful, driven from the upper air,
By torchlight share the Holy Mysteries,
And nerve themselves to face the cunning pains

Of fiercest torture. Oh, that the day may come
When I, as they, may welcome martyrdom !

Enter MARCUS.

MARCUS.

Most Holy Father, Leonidas is here ;
And brings a stranger with him who desires
To speak with thee.

URBAN.

Let them come in, my son.
[*Exit Marcus.*

Enter VALERIAN *and* LEONIDAS.

LEONIDAS.

I know not, Holy Father, whom I've brought
To visit you ; he will announce himself.
He comes from Lady Cecily : that alone
I know will find him welcome.

URBAN.

Noble sir,

How can I serve you ?

VALERIAN.

I know and know not :
I feel that thou canst give me happiness ;
How thou'rt to give it me, I cannot tell.

URBAN.

Leave us alone, my son Leonidas ;
God bless you ! [*Exit Leonidas.*] Now, my lord, you
        bring me news
From Lady Cecily.
                    VALERIAN.
                    From her, my spouse.

URBAN.

Then thou art Lord Valerian ?

VALERIAN.

I am he.

URBAN.

This day was fixed to be your wedding-day.

VALERIAN.

It was ; and we are wed.   But I am come
For matter of more moment e'en than that.

Cecilia is a Christian ; and she speaks
Words of such wondrous import, that I feel
The God she worships must be very God ;
And what she holds, the truth.   I am come
To be instructed, Father.

URBAN [*kneels*].

Gracious God !
Fountain of good, the Source of chaste desires !
Thou hast Thyself implanted in the heart
Of Cecily the seed from whence has sprung
This fruit of blessing.   Shepherd of the sheep !
The work Thou gavest Cecily, she has done.
[*Rises*]   Valerian came, a lion in his strength,
In every gift of nature lacking nought,
But looking still for glory among men.
She has restored him to Thee, wholly weaned
From love of worldly glare, content to learn
The Cross of Christ and meek humility.
Already he believes the Christian faith ;
Open his heart to faith more perfect still,
That, listed 'neath the banner of the Cross,
He may renounce the devil and his works—
A faithful soldier of the Crucified !

VALERIAN.

God of the Christians, hear! Oh, give me light!
God, I believe! Oh, help my want of faith!

Enter St. Peter. Valerian *on his knee.*

St. PETER.

Son of election!   Saints on earth, in heaven,
Are interceding for thee.   Christ, the Son
Of the Eternal Father, hears their prayer:
'Tis He hath sent me to thee.   Arise my son:

[*Valerian rises.*

Read here the words of everlasting life,
Written in gold.

VALERIAN [*reads*].

" One Lord, one faith, one baptism : one Lord and
Father of all, Who is above all, and through all,
and in us all."

St. PETER.

Believe in God the Father, Who hath made thee;
Believe in God the Son, Who died for thee;
Believe in God the Holy Ghost, Whose power
Shall make thee child of God.—Urban, to thee
I leave the rest.   The peace of God upon you!

[*Exit.*

URBAN.

Amen! Valerian, thou believest all
The Prince of the Apostles, whom thine eyes
Have seen, hath told thee?

VALERIAN.

Nothing more truly: I believe it all.

URBAN.

"One Lord, one faith, one *baptism.*" There remains
Only to wash thee in the cleansing flood
Of holy baptism. Come with me, my son:
God shall complete the work He hath begun.

END OF THE SECOND ACT.

ACT THE THIRD.

SCENE I.

Ualerian's Palace.

CECILIA *and* AZRAEL.

CECILIA.

I FEEL I cannot pray; my inmost soul
Is tuned to strains of joyful thanksgiving;
My heart exults with joy.   O Azrael!
Is it not true my spouse is won to God,
And made a Christian?

AZRAEL.

      He comes, my charge,
To speak himself.

VALERIAN.

Praise to the living God!
My spouse, I am a Christian. [*Sees Azrael.*]   Ah
blessed Spirit,

My eyes behold thee now ; and I confess
The watchful care of God for Cecily.

CECILIA.

My heart will burst with happiness and joy !
Oh, be Thou praised, O God !   You too rejoice,
Ye blessed Saints and Spirits, who have prayed
And won your prayer !

AZRAEL.

Children dear !
Brother and sister in the heart of God ;
I bring you from the gardens of the blest
These garlands sent to you by Jesus Christ.
He bids me say how much He loves you both :
How much He'd have you love each other.   See !
The garlands are of roses mixed with lilies :
The lily figures your chaste mutual love ;
The rose foreshadows grace of martyrdom.
Besides, Valerian, on this happy day—
Thy birthday to a better, endless life—
Thy Lord would have thee choose whate'er thou
        wilt,
And He will grant it you.

VALERIAN.

My choice is made:
I have a brother whom I love, blest Spirit,
As my own soul.   I pray that my Tiburtius
May, like myself, embrace the faith of Christ.

AZRAEL.

The Lord approves thy choice.   Tiburtius
Shall, through thy prayers and Cecily's, receive
The gift of faith.   Nay, what is more, Tiburtius
Shall with Valerian seal his faith in blood;
And o'er your relics, shall, in times to come,
The Holy Sacrifice be offered up.
Farewell, my children; time is hastening on;
Soon shall you join me in the heavenly home.

[Exit.

SCENE II.

The Court.

Turcius Almachius *alone.*

ALMACHIUS.

WHAT swarms there are of these same Christian
vermin !
I thought that yesterday might bring an end ;
But still there seems no ending.

Enter Lucius *and* Mucro.

Who are you,
Come in such haste ?

LUCIUS.

My lord, Valerian
Proclaims himself a Christian.

ALMACHIUS.

Nonsense, man !
Valerian a Christian ?   Who has dared
To spread so vile a tale ?

LUCIUS.

Nay, 'tis a fact.
While I was ferreting the noxious brutes

Out of the quarter of the Aventine,
I met Valerian, and Tiburtius too,
Dispensing alms, encouraging the slaves,
And urging them to bear with constancy
The persecution, as they're pleased to call
Thy enterprise in favour of the gods.

ALMACHIUS.

Why, this is news indeed will startle Rome.
Can it be true?   'Twas only yesterday
He sent rich gifts to Juno Pronuba,
In honour of his marriage.

LUCIUS.

              Here's a man
Will tell you more about it.

ALMACHIUS.

              Who are you?

MUCRO.

My name is Mucro; Valerian my master.

ALMACHIUS.

And art thou able to bear out the charge
That Lucius has made?

MUCRO.

I am, my lord, and more :
I came to prove my faithfulness to Rome
And the immortal gods. I take it ill
That Lucius should pretend to be the first,
And snatch from me the merit of the deed.

ALMACHIUS.

It matters little. Valerian is rich,
And he shall pay you both.

MUCRO.

'Tis just, my lord ;
But I have more to tell. The Lady Cecily
Is likewise of the sect : Valerian's slaves
Hermes and Soter ; Charis too and Maura,
Slaves of Metellus' household—all refuse
To offer incense to the immortal gods.

ALMACHIUS.

What leads thee, Mucro, to accuse thy master?

MUCRO.

That matters little, so my tale be true ;

F

And less when you consider as its fruit
The wealth of Lord Valerian and his spouse.

ALMACHIUS.

Slaves will be mercenary ; go, you shall receive
Fitting reward for your fidelity :
I will consider how most prudently
We may avenge the honour of the gods.

[*Exeunt Lucius and Mucro.*

ALMACHIUS [*alone*].

" The honour of the gods "—such is the plea
For persecuting Christians to the death ;
And such is mine : but of all the gods
Plutus most pleases me, the god of wealth.
And "slaves are mercenary"—oh, yes ! that's true,
Because their gains are small ; but as for me,
Why, 'tis a virtue to despoil a man
Like this Valerian ; for the gain is great.
If there are gods, they will not punish me
For doing what their godships do themselves :
If there are none, why, then there's none to punish ;
So either way I'm safe.   Or good, or bad,
I'm like to drive a profitable trade.   [*Exit.*

SCENE III.

Valerian's Palace.

CECILIA *alone.*

CECILIA.

THE end is fast approaching. Heaven above
Waits but to welcome us. Valerian's heart
Finds correspondence in his open hand,
Gladdens the widow and the orphan, bids
Sorrow rejoice and poverty be rich.
Did I not say he'd make a noble Christian?
Tiburtius too is ours! God's mighty grace
Has in the earliest hours of conversion
Made them mature at once, like Adam sprung
Adult and perfect from the virgin earth.
This cannot be for nothing : already ripe,
God will ere long complete His gracious work.
And house them in His heavenly garner.

Enter CHARIS *and* MAURA.

CHARIS.

Sister,
Valerian and Tiburtius, Soter, Hermes,

F 2

Have been arrested by Almachius' order,
And dragged before him.

CECILIA.

I did expect such news;
And is this all?

CHARIS.

Mucro, Valerian's slave,
Appeared against them.   Miserable man!
No sooner was the judgment passed, but he
Fell in a fit, stone dead.

CECILIA.

Alas, poor man!
This only mars our joy.   They were condemned?

CHARIS.

Yes, all of them: Hermes, young in faith,
Seemed once to waver; but Valerian laid
His hand upon his head, and bade him think
Of Him Who in the morning had reposed
Within his bosom.   Valerian's touch
Seemed tò infuse new courage: Hermes
Flinched not again—was constant to the last;
Masters and slaves were brethren in their death.

CECILIA.

What, Charis! are they really put to death,
And you delayed to tell me of the best?

CHARIS.

The flesh is weak, dear sister, and I knew
How much thou lov'dst Valerian; so I feared
To announce at once their glorious martyrdom.

CECILIA.

Thou'rt ever thoughtful, Charis; but in this
I feel my weakness so upheld by grace,
I cannot weep unless it be for joy.

MAURA.

O God, how dost Thou prove Thyself alone
The Great, the Good, the Beautiful, the True,
By the great works Thou workest in Thy Saints!

CHARIS.

Be of good cheer, dear Maura: thou and I,
Like Soter and his fellow, will attend
Our dearest mistress on her way to bliss
As they their honoured masters.

MAURA.

I am weak,
And a mere neophyte : my will is good,
But insecure as Hermes', and I beg
Thee, my dear mistress, to remember me,
And help me as Valerian did him.

Enter LEONIDAS.

LEONIDAS.

Lady Cecilia——

CECILIA.

Nay, good Leonidas,
Thou art behindhand ; I have heard the news :
We have four intercessors more in Heaven.

LEONIDAS.

Four intercessors, lady?   Then thou hast not heard
All that I had to tell.   Thy spouse has led
A gallant troop to bear him company.
The Prefect gave to Maximus, his chamberlain,
Charge to conduct the execution.   He,
Touched with the constancy of the four thou knowest,
Professed himself a Christian, and some thirty more,
Who had gone forth the ministers of Satan,

Offered to bear the death they came to give.
Bravely they stood the mockery and jeers
Of their companions ; and amid a shower
Of scourges, loaded with lead bullets, sealed
Their new-won faith in baptism of blood.

CECILIA.

Good is in store for us : I have long wished
To change this world of shadows, and behold
That which alone deserves the name of real.
Now is my longing stronger ; for the stroke
That severs me from earth will reunite
Me and my husband and Tiburtius.
But we are wasting time.   We cannot pray
For martyrs ; but we can perform their will,
And add another splendour to their crown.
We will assemble all the poor of Rome ;
And spread abroad, on this high festal day,
With lavish hand, the treasures of my spouse.
We will spare nothing ; for the wealth was his,
And his shall be the merit of its use.

SCENE IV.

𝕿𝖍𝖊 𝕳𝖔𝖚𝖘𝖊 𝖔𝖋 𝕬𝖑𝖒𝖆𝖈𝖍𝖎𝖚𝖘.

ALMACHIUS; *enter to him* LUCIUS.

LUCIUS.

THE Lady Cecily is arrested ; what
Are your commands ?

ALMACHIUS.

You may bring her in.

[*Exit Lucius.*

Now to secure my prize.   I've ventured much
In speculation lately, and my coffers
Need a new filling.   Nothing could have chanced
So happily as this : I shall begin to grow
Devout to Mercury.   Most of these Christian dogs
Turn out so poor that they're not worth the killing ;
But here's a game worth catching.   Here she comes.

Enter LUCIUS, *with* CECILIA, CHARIS, MAURA.

Lady Cecilia, I would fain believe
The rumours spread about thee to be false :

Thy noble forefathers have well deserved
Of Rome and of the Emperors. The gods
Have found in them devoted worshippers,
And thou art heir to all their noble deeds.
Say thou art not a Christian and depart
Safe and unhurt.

CECILIA.

My lord, I am a Christian.

ALMACHIUS.

Recall the word ; I would deal gently with thee ;
For thou art young and beautiful, and Rome
Resounds with thy fair fame.

CECILIA.

I am a Christian.

ALMACHIUS.

A Christian, lady ? Can that odious sect
Have trapped thee in its snares ?

CECILIA.

The Christian faith

Teaches the love of one Eternal God,
And love to man : why should it be odious ?

ALMACHIUS.

The Christian faith refuses to adore
The gods of Rome.

CECILIA.

The gods of Rome, my lord,
Have nought to recommend them.   They them-
selves,
If they are anything, are headlong dragged
By hateful passion to do deeds of shame
Their worshippers would blush at.

ALMACHIUS.

Thou art not
Fit to dispute on matters such as these :
Thy fathers have for many generations
Worshipped the gods : thou lackest modesty
To censure them.

CECILIA.

They from whom at first
Those fathers sprang who worshipped the false gods,
Worshipped the only true and living God.
I but resume the holy faith which they
My fathers forfeited.

ALMACHIUS.

I am not here
To argue, Lady Cecily, but to enforce
That which the State acknowledgeth as right.
Lucius, prepare the incense.   Bethink thee, lady :
If thou refuse to throw the grain of incense
Into the brazier, as submission's sign,
There but remains for thee, as for the rest,
Who number now five thousand, certain death.
Have pity on thyself.   Behold the brazier !
Hand her the incense.   Lady, you refuse ?
Escape is none : Tiburtius is dead ;
Valerian is dead ; and thou must die.

CECILIA.

My lord, Valerian lives ; Tiburtius lives ;
And I, that I may live, do long to die.

ALMACHIUS.

Riddles and frenzy !   Lucius, who are these
Who stand with Cecily ?

LUCIUS.

Slaves, my lord, suspected
Of being Christians too.

ALMACHIUS.

What are your names ?

CHARIS.

My name is Charis.

MAURA.

And my name is Maura.

ALMACHIUS.

Charis and Maura, take the grains of incense,
And burn them to the god.

CHARIS.

This god is none.

MAURA.

The God of Christians is the only God.

ALMACHIUS.

Then you shall share your mistress' punishment.
But, one word, lady.   I have pity for you,
And would fain save you.   The Emperor has need
Of means to carry on his Government,
And all men know Valerian was rich.
If you will tell me where to find his wealth,

That I may use it for the public good,
I will hush up the matter, and release
You and your slaves.   'Twas for this, indeed,
I did prefer to examine you in private,
And did not summon you in open court.

CECILIA.

Almachius, you profess a kindly heart,
And may God bless you as you do intend it.
But it is all too late : Valerian's wealth
Has been deposited in a treasure-house
You cannot reach.
ALMACHIUS.
Nay, Lady Cecily,
Trust me for that.   I've friends in every province,
And I can use the strong hand of the law
To enforce my will.
CECILIA.
Valerian's wealth
I have distributed among the poor,
And there is nought reserved.

ALMACHIUS.
Say you so ?
Then it is plain that thou art criminal,

And traitress to the State.   Long and wearisome
Shall be thy death.   Take away the slaves,
Despatch them instantly.

CHARIS *and* MAURA *kneel before* CECILIA, *who blesses them.*

CECILIA.

Sisters in Christ,
God bless you !

ALMACHIUS.

Away with them, away !
You, treacherous dame, shall in your own palace
Die ling'ring, stifled in the bath.   Lucius,
See to these orders : have them straight obeyed.
Away with them !

[*Exeunt all but Almachius.*

Plague on these Christian dogs !
My only chance of mending my affairs
Baffled and crost !   This is the return
The gods bestow on my fidelity !
Plague on the gods !   Confusion on myself !

SCENE V.

The Bath in Cecilia's Palace.

CECILIA, MARCUS, CHRISTIANS.

CECILIA.

MARCUS, the time is short: peace is at
    hand;
And I will pray for thee and for all Rome
When it shall please my Spouse to call
    me hence.

MARCUS.

Urban will soon be here: I sent for him
Some two hours gone.

CECILIA.

       God bless thee, Marcus, for it!
I fain would see my Father ere I die.

MARCUS.

I think I hear him coming. There is one
Just now arrived: the footsteps are familiar,
And must be his.

Enter URBAN.

URBAN.

My child ! my martyred child !

CECILIA.

Bless me, my Father.

URBAN.

God Almighty bless thee !

CECILIA.

And thou art come to close thy daughter's eyes.
I felt that thou would'st come : so many graces
Has God bestowed through thee, this last one too
Thou shalt, on this my happy birthday, be
God's minister in giving ; from thy hands
Christ shall receive me as His spouse for ever.

URBAN.

Thou hast dealt hardly with me, Cecily :
Thou hast deprived me of the martyr's crown,
And wearest it thyself ; yet, I am old—
Thou, in the spring-tide of thy virgin life.'
Alas ! the oldest are not therefore ripest :
I, old in years, and thou in charity.

But rest awhile, my child ; my coming in
Hath slightly moved thee. When our Marcus here
Hath told the manner of thy suffering,
Thou shalt declare to me the special cause
Why thou didst wish so urgently to see me.

MARCUS.

No sooner had Almachius pronounced
The sentence which secured Cecilia
The crown of martyrdom, but his officers
Led her with furious haste across the Tiber
To this her house. The furnaces that heated
Her private bath were kindled, and the chamber
Secured from entrance of the outward air.
Roughly the menials performed their part ;
And 'mid the tears of strangers and of friends,
Thrusting their victim through the opened door,
Left her to die. A day and night had passed
Before again the bath was opened. Then,
Instead of finding a misshapen corse,
Dried up and shrivelled, to their wondering eyes
Cecilia lay, as though in sweetest sleep,
Fresh and unharmed. When the brute element
Had thus refused to execute its office

G

On God's elect, then the freewill of man
Was summoned to complete the sacrifice.
Three times the headsman aimed his deadly blow;
Three times he failed to sever from the trunk
The virgin's head ; and so he left her lying,
E'en as you see her now, thus welling forth
Her life-blood in one lengthened martyrdom.
Her living death has cast a spell on Rome :
Almachius is gone ; and friends and foes
Gather around the holy virgin, while
The persecutor sheathes the sword in fear.

URBAN.

'Tis a long death thou sufferest, my daughter ;
But every moment of thy agony
Shall win thee higher bliss.

CECILIA.

                       'Tis sweet to die
For Him Who died for me.   But now, my Father,
The time of my departure is at hand.
I did desire to see thee, to implore
A favour of thee.   Make this house of mine
A temple of the true and living God.
I leave thee all I have : dispose of all—

First, for God's public worship : what remains,
Distribute to the poor.

URBAN.

It shall be done :
And when thou standest in the sight of God,
Crowned with the coronet for virgins kept,
Bearing the martyr's palm-branch in thy hand,
Pray for thy Father Urban, and for Rome.

CECILIA.

O happy birthday to eternal bliss !
Glory to Father, Son, and Holy Ghost !
I come, Valerian ! Mother of God, I come !
Into Thy Hands, O God, I yield my spirit !

[Dies.

URBAN.

Farewell, thou favourite of Heaven ! We say
No prayer for thee, but bid thee pray for us.
See how her hands proclaim the holy faith
In which she lived and died—the faith she spoke
In the last words she uttered ! On her breast
One finger of the left hand lies across
Three of the right. Though dead, she speaketh still :
Three Persons and one God for ever blest !

G 2

SCENE VI.

Glory of the Saints.

CECILIA, VALERIAN, AZRAEL, CHARIS, MAURA, SOTER, HERMES, ST. PETER *and* URBAN, LEONIDAS, MARCUS, *&c.*

Hymn of St. Cecilia.

GOD, Father, Son, and Spirit,
   And God-Man crucified,
The faith that we inherit,
   Faith of the martyr bride.

Chorus.

While ages course along,
Prais'd be, with tuneful song,
Blest Cecily, the martyr bride,
   By ev'ry heart and tongue.

She caught the living fire
   With rapturous love that glowed
In Heaven's seraphic choir,
   Around the throne of God.

No bee from fragrant heather
   So deftly stored its cell,

As she, God's praise to gather,
  From every theme had skill.

'Mid Pagan acclamation
  That hailed her marriage-feast,
Her heart mused on the Passion
  And death of Jesus Christ.

Her gold-embroidered clothing
  A hair-shirt underlay;
Her soul shrank back with loathing
  From Gentile revelry.

An Angel brought the spouses
  In either hand a wreath :
White lilies and red roses—
  Virginity and Death!

MISCELLANEOUS HYMNS.

COR JESU.

DEM Herzen Jesu singe
Mein Herz in Liebeswonn'!
Durch alle Wolken dringe
Der laute Jubelton.

Chorus.

Gelobt, gebenedeit
Soll sein zu jeder Zeit
Das heiligste Herz Jesu
In alle Ewigkeit.

O Herz für mich gebrochen
Aus übergrosser Huld
Von einer Lanz' durchstochen
Ob meiner Sündenschuld!

O Herz, in lauter Flammen
Von Liebe ganz verzehrt
In dieses Herzen's Namen
Wird Alles mir gewährt.

COR JESU.

To JESUS' Heart all burning
  With fervent love for men,
My heart with fondest yearning
  Shall raise its joyful strain.

Chorus.

While ages course along,
  Blest be with loudest song,
The Sacred Heart of Jesus,
  By every heart and tongue.

O Heart, for sinners riven
  By sheer excess of love,
The spear thro' Thee was driven,
  'Twas sin of mine that drove.

O Heart, for me on fire
  With love no tongue can speak,
My yet untold desire
  God gives me for Thy sake.

Herr Jesu! Eine Bitte—
Nur Eins verlang' ich hier,
In deines Herzen's Mitte
Gib auch ein Plätzchen mir.

Zwar bin ich voller Sünden,
Ein Lamm, das sich verirrt,
Doch sieh', ich lass mich finden
Von dir, O guter Hirt.

O wasche meine Seele
Mit deines Herzen's Blut,
Zur Braut sie dann erwähle
O allerhöchstes Gut!

Wie du von Herzen milde
Und demuthsvoll und rein,
So soll nach deinem Bilde
Mein Herz gestaltet sein.

Hinweg mit allen Trieben
Worin die Welt sich freut,
Nur Jesum will ich lieben,
Ihm sei mein Herz geweiht.

Dear Lord, my soul would venture
  To urge one earnest prayer,
Keep, Lord, in Thy Heart's centre,
  One little nook for her.

Too true I have forsaken
  Thy hearth by wilful sin ;
Yet let me now be taken
  Back to my home again.

From all that can infect me,
  O cleanse me with Thy Blood ;
For Thine own spouse elect me,
  My God! my Sovereign Good !

As Thou art meek and lowly,
  And ever pure of heart,
So may my heart be wholly
  Of Thine the counterpart.

Away with earthly passion,
  Away with sordid pelf.
In my heart's consecration,
  I yield Thee all myself.

Wer gibt mir Taubenflügel
Zu Jesu Herzen hin,
Dass über Berg und Hügel
Zu Ihm ich möge flieh'n!

In dieses Herzen's Wunde
Ist meiner Seele Ruh',
In Glück und Leidesstunde
Ruf' ich der Welt dann zu.

Und wenn die Augen brechen,
Entflieht der Erde Schein,
Will ich noch sterbend sprechen
Herz Jesu, ich bin dein.

Would that to me were given
   The pinions of the dove,
I'd pierce the highest heaven
   My Jesus' love to prove.

Within the cleft I'll cower,
   Of Jesus' wounded side ;
In sunshine or in shower
   Securely there I'll hide.

When life away is flying,
   And earth's false glare is done,
Still, Sacred Heart, in dying,
   I'll say—" I'm all Thine own."

DIE NACHTIGALLEN SINGEN.

[G. Görres.]

Die Nachtigallen singen:
Der Mai ist froh erwacht
Drum wollen wir dir bringen
Was uns der Mai gebracht:
Und hier zu deinen Füssen
Mit Blumen dich begrüssen—
Maria, O Maria.

O Jungfrau dein Erbarmen
Verschmäht die Blumen nicht
Die dir die Hand des Armen
Zum Kranze liebend pflicht:
Du hör'st den Ruf der Schmerzen,
Drum rufen wir von Herzen—
Maria, O Maria.

Wir bringen dir die Blüthen
Für unser Herz als Pfand,
O wolle uns behüten
Mit treuer Mutter-hand:
Das wir in deinem Schoosse
Erblühen gleich der Rose—
Maria, O Maria.

THE QUEEN OF MAY.

[*From* G. Görres.]

The nightingales are singing,
  Sweet harbingers of May,
And many a flower is springing,
  Or opening to the day:
Shall we be slow to meet thee,
With flowers and hymns to greet thee
  Mary, Mother dear?

Never, O gentlest maiden,
  Hast thou been known to scorn
Wreath from the sorrow-laden
  Or plaint of the forlorn:
To thee our heart rejoices,
To thee we tune our voices—
  Mary, Mother dear.

We bring thee gifts of flowers
  Our childlike love to prove;
Guard, when the tempest lowers,
  Our hearts with careful love:
And we sometime shall blossom
Like roses in thy bosom—
  Mary, Mother dear.

O du in Gottes Garten
Als Gärtnerin bestellt,
Beschirm uns vor den harten
Gefahren dieser Welt—
Dass uns der Feind nicht schade
Im Schatten deiner Gnade,
Maria, O Maria.

Maria! Gnadenbronne,
Bethaue unser Herz,
Du klare Himmels-sonne,
Verkläre Lust und Schmerz,
Und lass uns, eh' wir sterben,
Den Himmelsgarten erben,
Maria, O Maria.

Und wann auf deinen Auen
Der Himmelsmai erblüht,
O Jungfrau der Jungfrauen,
Sei gnadenvoll bemüht,
Dass wir mit Maienzweigen
Dann singen in dem Reigen,
Maria, O Maria.

'Tis thine the flowers to cherish
  In God's fair garden set;
Too surely we should perish,
  Could'st thou thy love forget:
But thou wilt ne'er forsake us,
Nor scath nor foe o'ertake us—
    Mary, Mother dear.

Thou hast by God been chosen,
  With radiance clear and warm,
To melt our hearts so frozen,
  And mould them into form:
Then, weaned from joys forbidden,
Transplant us into Eden—
    Mary, Mother dear.

When, in those fields of azure,
  May shall in Heaven unfold,
Within that safe enclosure
  Our hands fair wreaths shall hold,
And while thou smilest o'er us
We'll sing in joyful chorus—
    Mary, Mother dear.

II

SEQUENTIA DE BEATA MARIA VIRGINE SINE LABE CONCEPTA.

[CARD. GEISSEL.]

VIRGO Virginum præclara,
Præter omnes Deo cara,
  Dominatrix cœlitum.

Fac nos pie te cantare,
Prædicare et amare,
  Audi vota supplicum.

Quis est dignus, laude digna
Collaudare te benigna
  Virgo, fons charismatum?

Gratiis es tota plena,
Tota pulchra, lux serena,
  Dei tabernaculum.

O quam magna tibi fecit,
Qui est potens, et adjecit
  Gratiam ad gratiam!

Qui cœlum terramque regit,
Matrem sibi te selegit,
  Sponsam atque filiam.

SEQUENCE FOR THE FEAST OF THE IMMACULATE CONCEPTION.

[*From* CARD. GEISSEL.]

VIRGIN of all virgins highest,
Virgin to God's heart the nighest,
  Queen enthroned above the sky :

May our bosoms love thee well,
May our tongues thy praises tell,
  Hear, O hear, thy suppliants' cry.

Who hath skill with praise condign
Thee to praise, O maid benign,
  Fountain of the gifts of grace ?

Thou of grace art wholly full,
Calmly bright, all beautiful,
  And God's chosen dwelling-place.

Truly He, the mighty One,
Hath to thee great wonders done,
  Thee with grace on grace endows :

He, who ruleth heaven and earth,
Chooseth thee to give Him birth,
  His own Mother, Daughter, Spouse.

H 2

Virgo, vere benedicta,
Culpa nunquam es obstricta
  Carnis in exilio.

Sine labe tu concepta,
Magno lapsui prærepta,
  Summo privilegio.

Contendebat certatura
Tunc cum Gratia Natura,
  Gratia prævaluit.

A peccato præservatam
Immunem et illibatam
  Mire te constituit.

Eva nova novæ legis,
Præelecta summi Regis,
  Consors ejus gloriæ,

Tu draconem domuisti,
Forti pede contrivisti
  Victrix caput Satanæ.

Semper fulgens munda stola,
Inter mundas munda sola,
  Ascendisti sidera ;

Virgin blest in very deed,
Though this exile world thou tread,
  Sin no bands can cast on thee ;

Thou conceiv'd all clear of stain,
From the general ruin ta'en,
  Privileged ineffably.

Nature, loath to yield her prey,
Hasted eagerly that day,
  Hand to hand with grace to strive :

Grace hath won, and thou within
Art all spotless kept from sin—
  Wonderful prerogative !

Thou, the New Law's better Eve,
Wast predestined to receive
  Glory with th' Eternal King :

Mightily we've seen thee tread
On the vanquished dragon's head ;
  Peals of triumph round thee ring.

Stainless did thy robe endure ;
Mid the pure, the only pure,
  Thou hast climbed the starry height :

Super agmina sanctorum,
Super choros angelorum
  Sceptra geris Domina.

Oras nunc a dextris Nati,
Jugo solvat ut peccati,
  Quos redemit sanguine ;

Manus tuæ stillant dona,
Vitæ fac cœlestis bona
  Et in nos defluere.

Esto nobis maris stella,
Ne nos fluctuum procella
  Navigantes obruat ;

Ex qua salus est exorta,
Esto nobis Cœli porta,
  Quæ salvandis pateat.

Virgo clemens, virgo pia,
Duc salutis nos in via
  Vitæ per exilium ;

Nos, O Mater, hic tuere,
Olim istic fac videre
  Te tuumque Filium.

High above the Saints in love,
High the Angel choirs above,
    Queen thou reign'st with sceptre bright.

Now, thou pray'st thy Son to break
Sin's hard yoke for sinners' sake,
    Whom by death He would redeem:

Graces from thy hands distil,
At thy instance blessings will
    Down on us in torrents stream.

Be to us the ocean star,
Lest, mid winds and waves at war,
    Our inconstant bark be riven:

Day-Spring, whence salvation rose,
When life's pilgrimage shall close,
    Be to us the gate of Heaven.

Virgin meek and Virgin mild,
While we tread this mazy wild,
    Be thy safe protection shown:

Here, defend us as we go,
There the happy sight bestow
    Of thyself and of thy Son.

Fac, te duce, nos orare,
Vigilare et certare,
  Certos tuæ gratiæ ;

Funde nobis pia dona,
Custos, mater et patrona
  Sanctæ sis Ecclesiæ.

Fac nos stare fide vera,
Charitate, spe sincera,
  Absque culpæ macula ;

Gregem Tibi sic dicatum,
Jam a patribus sacratum
  Protegas in sæcula.—Amen.

Sure of thy befriending aid,
We will in thy footsteps tread,
   And will watch and pray and strive:

From on high thy favours pour,
Patron, Mother, evermore
   To Christ's Church protection give.

Bid our hearts stand fast in faith,
Hope, and charity till death,
   By no hideous sin-spot marred:

So Christ's fold be thy own dow'r
(As our fathers willed of yore),
   Ever safe beneath thy guard.—Amen.

ST. PETER AND ST. PAUL.

[Printed in the *Omaggio Cattolico*, on the eighteenth centenary of
their martyrdom.]

"THOU art the Christ, the only Son of God."
Such was thine answer, Peter, to thy Lord ;
And He pronounced thee blest, for flesh and blood
Could not have taught thee. Then He spake the
    word—
" I name thee Rock, and on this Rock I will
Build my Church proof against the powers of hell."

Chorus.

All praise to Jesus Christ for Peter's Chair ;
He that would find the truth will find it there.

One with thy brethren, Peter, thou, like them,
Art laid with strength as firm as adamant—
Foundation of the new Jerusalem :
But thou art more, for, by thy Lord's intent,
Partaking in His right, and by His call,
Thou art the Rock that underlies them all.

Prince of the Apostles !   For to thee was given
The symbol of God's Kingdom amongst men ;

The keys to close or ope the gates of Heaven,
To bind or loose, as chiefest sovereign.
What thou shalt tie on earth, in Heaven is tied ;
What thou shalt loose, as loosed is ratified.

Satan desired to have the Apostles all,
To winnow them like wheat before the wind :
But Christ hath prayed for one, that none might fall
Whose faith by Peter's should be countersigned.
Then praised be Jesus Christ for Peter's Chair ;
He who would find the truth will find it there.

Hail, blessed Rome, where Peter's self unfurled
The standard of the Cross, and mighty Paul,
Doctor of Gentiles, master of the world,
Announced Christ's triumph, and the idols' fall :.
Rome, on whose shore the twin Apostles died,
Paul by the sword and Peter crucified.

[We needs must love thee, Peter, for thou wast
Our father's healer on his bed of pain ;
What wonder by a vow, our fourth and last,
He would his children to thy fealty chain ;
Still tend to us, his sons, thy loving care,
And make us worthy Jesus' name to bear.]

THE HOLY CROSS.

Hail, O sacred Rood,
Purpled with the Blood
Of Him Who suffered for mankind on thee,
Standard of the Cross,
Raised on high for us,
Lead the hosts of Christ to victory.

Mighty work of God,
When upon the Rood
Life upyielded life, and death did die.
We are sinking fast,
Like Peter 'neath the blast ;
Cross of Christ, to thee for aid we cry,
Hail, O sacred Rood !

Spirits that resist
God's anointed Christ
Fly before the Cross's vengeful might :
By the blessed Rood
Ye shall be withstood,
Weakness shall be strong and brave your spite :
Hail, O sacred Rood !

O most blessed tree,
Jesus nailed to thee,
Made death the passage to the port of rest.
Heaven then forbid
We boast of aught beside
Thee—the blood-stained Cross of Jesus Christ:
Hail, O sacred Rood!

HYMN OF ST. AGNES.

BOOTLESS the tyrant's ire
The lamb-like child to quell;
In vain he lit the fire,
In vain he bared the steel.
While ages course along,
Praised be with sweetest song,
Agnes, the lamb-like martyr girl,
By every Christian tongue.

He swore with foul dishonour
To crush her maiden pride;
Her Master's seal was on her,
His Angel at her side.
While ages course along, &c.

Christ for His own had crowned her
  With pearls of matchless price,
And sparkling gems all round her
  Decked forth her sacrifice.
          While ages course along, &c.

The Christian maid unshaken
  The tyrant's rage defied ;
Her high resolve was taken
  To be no mortal's bride.
          While ages course along, &c.

The Pagans thronged about her,
  At sight of death unmoved ;
She smiled on him who smote her,
  And sped to Him she loved.
          While ages course along, &c.

Thou who wast strong in weakness
  And lovely without guile,
Pray that our Master's meekness
  Our hearts like thine may fill.
          While ages course along, &c.

NATIVITY OF THE BLESSED VIRGIN.

BRETHREN, see in Mary's birth
God Almighty's gift to earth,
Gift, the harbinger of spring,
Gift, forerunner of our King,
Beaming on mankind forgiven
Like the morning star in Heaven.
     Mary, Mother, born to-day,
     Pray for us thy children, pray.

God is in the gift He gives,
'Tis by God that Mary lives;
God in Mary gives her sense,
Gives in her, intelligence.
God in her, by grace divine,
Makes her His most cherished shrine.
     Mary, Mother, &c.

Nor does God inactive dwell
In the shrine He loves so well.
It is God that moves her heart
To take up the sinner's part;
God that makes her what she is,
Full of tenderest sympathies.
     Mary, Mother, &c.

He the exhaustless source supreme,
She the unexhausted stream,
He the sun, and she the ray,
He the ocean, she the spray,
He the light, the mirror she,
Dazzling to intensity.
                    Mary, Mother, &c.

Glory then to God in Heaven,
For the gift to creatures given,
Father, Son, and Holy Spirit,
Fount of grace and source of merit;
Praise to God, the Three in One,
For the grace to sinners done.
                    Mary, Mother, &c.

www.ingramcontent.com/pod-product-compliance
Lightning Source LLC
Chambersburg PA
CBHW030631270326
41927CB00007B/1390